IMAGES
of America

HISTORIC
BONAVENTURE
CEMETERY

PHOTOGRAPHS FROM THE COLLECTION OF
THE GEORGIA HISTORICAL SOCIETY

The Georgia Historical Society is headquartered in Hodgson Hall in Savannah. Hodgson Hall, named for William B. Hodgson, became the third home of the Society in September of 1875. The building was officially dedicated on February 14, 1876, and has been the Society's state-wide headquarters ever since. Housed within Hodgson Hall is one of the finest library collections of archives, manuscripts, photographs, books, and maps relating to the state of Georgia. The library is free and open to the public. Hodgson Hall is located at 501 Whitaker Street, Savannah, GA, 31499.

IMAGES
of America

HISTORIC
BONAVENTURE
CEMETERY

PHOTOGRAPHS FROM THE COLLECTION OF
THE GEORGIA HISTORICAL SOCIETY

Amie Marie Wilson
and Mandi Dale Johnson

ARCADIA

First printed 1998.
Reprinted 1999, 2000, 2001, 2002, 2003.

Published by Arcadia Publishing
an imprint of Tempus Publishing Inc.
Charleston SC, Chicago, Portsmouth NH, San Francisco

Printed in Great Britain

Library of Congress Catalog Card Number: 98-87702

For all general information contact Arcadia Publishing at:
Telephone 843-853-2070
Fax 843-853-0044
E-Mail sales@arcadiapublishing.com
For customer service and orders:
Toll-Free 1-888-313-2665

Visit us on the internet at http://www.arcadiapublishing.com

CONTENTS

THE GEORGIA HISTORICAL SOCIETY

Chartered by the Georgia Legislature in 1839, the Georgia Historical Society is a private, non-profit organization that serves as the historical society for the entire state of Georgia. For nearly 160 years, the Society has fulfilled its mission to collect, preserve, and share Georgia's history through the operation of its library and archives in Savannah. The Society exists to tell the story of our state's journey through time and to give our citizens a sense of whom we are as Georgians.

The Georgia Historical Society is headquartered in Savannah in historic Hodgson Hall and is a major research center serving approximately 16,000 researchers of Georgia history per year. Within the Society's library and archives is preserved one of the most outstanding collections of manuscripts, books, maps, photographs, newspapers, architectural drawings, portraits, and artifacts related to Georgia history anywhere in the country. The Society is continually adding to its collection through both donations and purchases.

In addition to its fabulous library, the Georgia Historical Society has an aggressive statewide outreach program. The Society accomplishes this mission in a variety of ways and to a wide audience. The Society conducts lectures and historical programs, administers the State Historical Marker Program, and most significantly, has a statewide Affiliate Chapter Program. This program is the foundation upon which all statewide outreach is built.

The Affiliate Chapter program encourages historical agencies and interested groups throughout the state to join the Georgia Historical Society in our mission to save Georgia history. Through this professional education program, the Society provides assistance, teaches workshops, and serves as an information clearinghouse for those historical agencies in need of help or advice. Staff members visit these organizations and conduct a consultation visit offering assistance in everything from archival management and administration to securing grant funds. The Affiliate Chapter Program, more specifically the workshops conducted as part of the program, were awarded the 1997 Professional Development Program of the Year by the Georgia Association of Museums and Galleries.

In addition to the Affiliate Chapter Program, the Georgia Historical Society anticipates a large statewide impact through the Georgia Heritage Celebration. This program, traditionally a Savannah event, has been turned over to the Georgia Historical Society. The 1999 Georgia Heritage Celebration will be taken to five pilot cities throughout the state and eventually is hoped to cover Georgia. The Georgia Heritage Celebration is held in February and is a time for us to remember the founding of our state. The program is directed at children and will be successful statewide with assistance of the Georgia Historical Society Affiliate Chapters and local boards of education.

The Georgia Historical Society also has an active publication program. The Society publishes the *Georgia Historical Quarterly* which is "The" magazine on Georgia History. The *Quarterly* is published in conjunction with the University of Georgia and has developed into one of the country's leading scholarly journals dedicated to a particular state. In 1840 the Society began publishing books with items from the collection. This is an ongoing activity at the Georgia Historical Society and this book is a continuation of that program.

INTRODUCTION

Bonaventure Cemetery is located 3 miles east of downtown Savannah, Georgia. The cemetery lies peacefully along the Wilmington River. Formerly a plantation, Bonaventure was turned into a cemetery shortly before the Civil War. Known for its moss-covered trees, colorful azaleas, and elaborate statuary, Bonaventure typifies cemeteries from the Victorian period.

With the rise of the middle class in the latter part of the 19th century, Americans' thoughts and ideas about death began to change. Death became romanticized and was often referred to as sleep. These views are reflected in the new cemeteries of the period. Elaborate grave markers and lush landscapes began to prevail. Even epitaphs reflected this change, often referring to the deceased as in "Silent Slumber" or "Sweet Repose." The overall atmosphere in Victorian cemeteries is one of hope.

In addition to the changes in the physical appearance of cemeteries, mourning became more ritualized during this period. Strict guidelines about mourning developed. These regulations governed every aspect of mourners' lives from their clothing to their accessories to their actions. With the development of embalming practices, the deceased could be put on display longer. Cosmetics were used to beautify the dead. Accompanying all this was the development of a separate profession to deal with funeral preparations as well as the creation of funeral parlors. The deceased were now displayed at these designated locations rather than in people's homes as they had before. This shielded the loved ones of the deceased from the gruesome task of handling the body after death. Elaborate caskets could now be purchased at the funeral homes. People were becoming separated from the morbid realities of death. They went to cemeteries for Sunday strolls and family picnics. Visits to cemeteries were no longer dreaded events.

Bonaventure Cemetery was bought by the City of Savannah in 1907. In 1937, the city acquired Greenwich, a neighboring plantation, and turned this into the Greenwich addition to Bonaventure. These cemeteries are run by the city's Park and Tree Commission.

This book provides a comprehensive visual record of this historical cemetery. It is divided into four parts. The chapters on Bonaventure and Greenwich focus on the history of these two former plantations and their transformation into cemeteries. The third chapter explores the lives of some of the people buried there. Chapter four, entitled "The Legacy," discusses sculptors' impact on Bonaventure and examines the cemetery's future.

The images used in this book come from the Georgia Historical Society's collections. The bulk of the images are from the Cordray-Foltz Collection (MS 1360) and the Georgia Historical Society Collection (MS 1361), while a few came from various family papers. Some of the images in Chapter 2 come from Mrs. Eleanor Torrey West's photograph album on deposit at the Georgia Historical Society. Also, included are several present-day photographs of the cemetery. These images are labeled as taken in 1998 and were photographed by the authors.

As an ideal Southern Victorian cemetery, Bonaventure has been well photographed. Although it is only one of many historic cemeteries in Savannah, Bonaventure is a real treasure. There is much of Savannah's, and Georgia's, history buried within its boundaries. We all need to do our part to ensure that this sacred burial ground is preserved for future generations to learn from and to enjoy.

ACKNOWLEDGMENTS

The authors wish to thank the staff of the Georgia Historical Society, particularly Assistant Director Frank Wheeler, for their help and patience during this undertaking. Thanks also go to Terry Shaw and Sarah Pinckney of the Bonaventure Historical Society for their help. We would like to commend their organization for the fine work they are doing to educate the public about this wonderful cemetery and to help preserve it. Finally, our thanks go to Abby Johnson for her assistance in photographing the cemetery.

This is the grave of Charles and Ernestine Seiler, Section A, lot 262. (Photograph taken by Frazier Smith in September 1962.)

One

BONAVENTURE

BONAVENTURE CEMETERY GATES, SAVANNAH, GA.

Bonaventure Cemetery was created in 1846 on the grounds of an 18th-century plantation that was originally the home of the Tattnall and Mullryne families. Between 1760 and 1765, Colonel John Mullryne and his son-in-law Josiah Tattnall, both of Beaufort, South Carolina, settled adjoining land along what is today St. Augustine's Creek. This land became known as Bonaventure, meaning "Good Fortune." This postcard of the entrance gates to the cemetery dates from around 1907.

Although the exact date of the marriage is unclear, Josiah Tattnall married Colonel Mullryne's daughter Mary, probably while they were still living in South Carolina. Supposedly, many of the old oak trees, for which Bonaventure Cemetery is famous, were planted in the shape of the letters "M" and "T" to commemorate this marriage between the Mullryne and Tattnall families. By 1771, Mullryne and Tattnall owned over 9,000 acres of land in south Georgia, stretching from Ebenezer to Sunbury.

During the Revolutionary War, Mullryne and Tattnall pledged their allegiance to King George III in 1775. The two men even helped Royal Governor James Wright escape his rebel captors. Wright fled Savannah to Bonaventure, where he boarded the ship *Scarborough* and made his way back to England. Mullryne and Tattnall would soon leave Georgia also, with Mullryne going to the Bahamas and Tattnall fleeing to England. Accused of treason by the Revolutionary Council in Savannah, their lands were confiscated and sold at auction in 1782. The 750 acres comprising Bonaventure were sold to John Habersham. Mullryne reportedly died in the Bahamas in 1786.

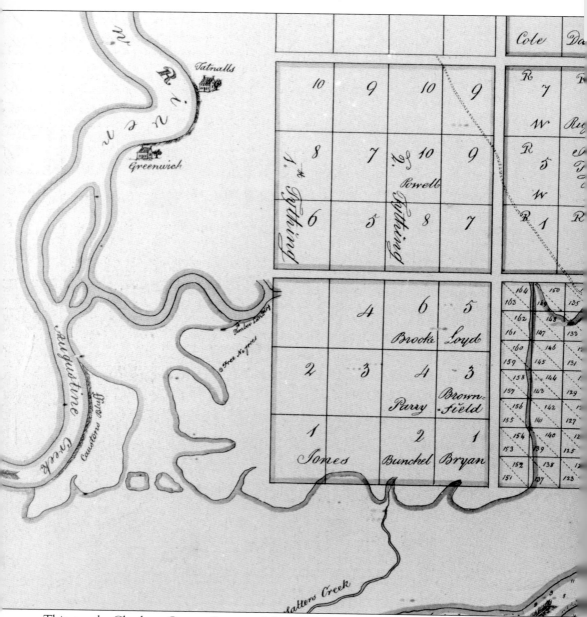

This map by Chatham County Surveyor John McKinnon shows Greenwich plantation and the home of the "Tatnalls" on what he called the Warsaw River (now the Wilmington River). The

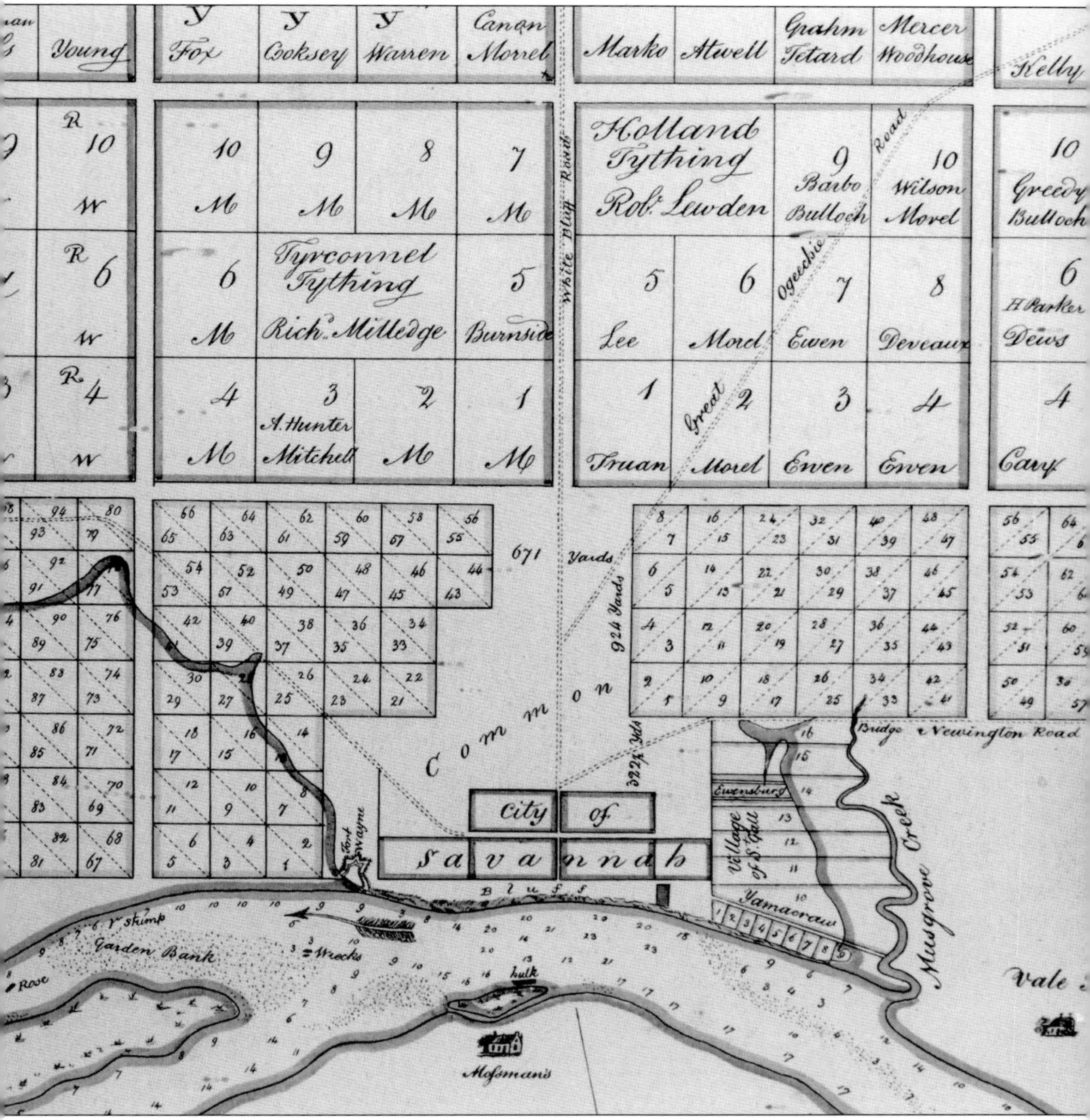

Map labels (top row, plantation/lot owners, left to right):
Young | Fox | Cooksey | Warren | Canon Morel | Marko | Atwell | Grahm Tetard | Mercer Woodhouse | Kelly

Grid content:

R 10 W | 10 M | 9 M | 8 M | 7 M | *Holland Tything* Robt. Lewden | 9 Barbo Bulloch | 10 Wilson Morel | 10 Greedy Bulloch

R 6 W | 6 M | *Tyrconnel Tything* Richd. Milledge | 5 Burnside | 5 Lee | 6 Morel | 7 Ewen | 8 Deveaux | 6 H.Parker Deirs

R 4 W | 4 M | A.Hunter 3 Mitchell | 2 M | 1 M | 1 Truan | 2 Morel | 3 Ewen | 4 Ewen | 4 Cary

White Bluff Road
Ogeechie Road
Great
671 Yards
924 Yards
Road

Numbered small lots (left block): 94 80 93 79 92 91 77 90 76 89 75 83 74 87 73 86 72 85 71 84 70 83 69 82 68 81 67 66 64 65 63 62 61 60 59 58 57 56 55 54 52 53 51 50 49 48 47 46 45 44 43 42 40 39 38 37 36 35 34 33 30 29 27 26 25 24 23 22 21 18 17 15 16 14 12 11 10 9 7 6 5 4 3 2 1

C o m m o n

Numbered lots (right block): 8 7 16 15 24 23 32 31 40 39 48 47 6 5 14 13 22 21 30 29 38 37 46 45 4 3 12 11 20 19 28 27 36 35 44 43 2 1 10 9 18 17 26 25 34 33 42 41 56 55 64 54 53 62 52 51 60 50 49 58 57

City of Savannah
Fort Wayne
Bluff

Village of St. Paul
Ewensburg
Bridge Newington Road
Musgrove Creek

16 15 14 13 12 11 10
Yamacraw 1 2 3 4 5 6 7 8

Garden Bank
Rose
Shrimp
Wrecks
hulk
Hofsman's
Vale

two plantations were located east of Savannah. The date of this map is unknown.

Josiah Tattnall Jr. returned to Savannah after the Revolutionary War and in 1785 bought back the Bonaventure property from John Habersham. Obviously, Josiah Jr. did not share his father's loyalist views. He introduced a new strain of sea island cotton from the Bahamas to Bonaventure and, in 1801, was elected governor of Georgia.

Josiah Tattnall Jr. married Harriet Fenwicke in 1786 in Savannah. The couple had three children live to adulthood—Edward Fenwick, Harriet, and Josiah III. The Tattnall's lives were not without tragedy, though. In 1802, Harriet died and was buried at Bonaventure beside her four children who died in infancy. The next year Josiah Jr. died in the Bahamas. He was buried beside his wife at Bonaventure. The plantation was left in trust to Josiah's three children, who were sent to live with their grandfather in London.

AVENUE IN BONAVENTURE CEMETERY, SAVANNAH, GA.

In 1817, Josiah Tattnall Jr.'s children reclaimed their family's lands. After his sister's death in 1819 and his brother's in 1832, Bonaventure passed solely to Commodore Josiah Tattnall III (1795–1871). Tattnall III joined the U.S. Navy in 1812. He had a distinguished naval career, fought in the Mexican War, and is reported to have been the author of the statement "Blood is thicker than water." He resigned his post in 1861 to offer his services to the Confederacy, which he served from 1861 to 1865. Commodore Tattnall died in Savannah in 1871 and was buried with his family at Bonaventure. The Tattnall family graves are located in what is today Section E, lot 1. (Photo taken April 1998.)

Since he lived most of his life at sea, Commodore Tattnall rarely spent time at Bonaventure. In 1846, he sold 600 acres of the family estate to Peter Wiltberger, a Savannah businessman and proprietor of the Pulaski House hotel, for $5,000. Two thousand dollars was to be paid directly to the St. Andrew's Society to settle a debt Commodore Tattnall had with them. The remainder was to be paid to the Commodore over a period of three years. The sale of Bonaventure excluded the Tattnall family cemetery, but Wiltberger agreed to maintain it. For unknown reasons, Wiltberger had plans to turn 70 acres of the property into a public cemetery.

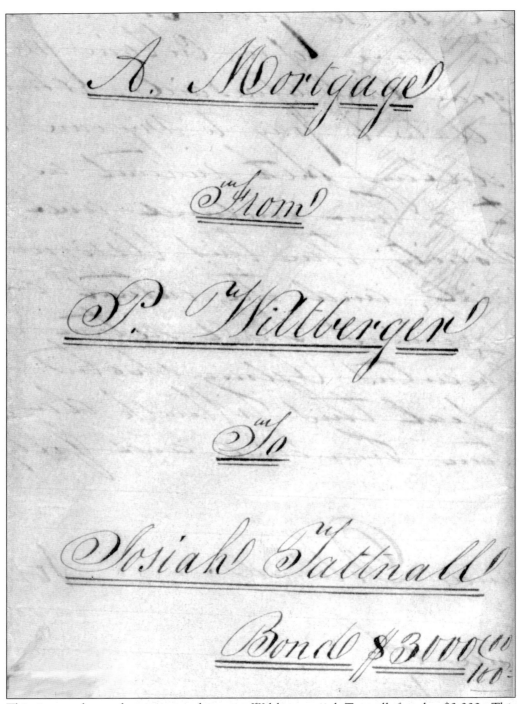

A. Mortgage

From

P. Wiltberger

To

Josiah Tattnall

Bond $3000 00/100

This image shows the mortgage between Wiltberger and Tattnall for the $3,000. This document is a part of the R.J. Davant Collection at the Georgia Historical Society.

Peter Wiltberger (1791–1853) died shortly after purchasing Bonaventure and was buried at the estate beside his wife Susan (1788–1849), and his son Rutherford (1827–1832). His other son, Major William Henry Wiltberger (1825–1872), pictured here, inherited his father's property. William joined the Confederate Army at the start of the Civil War as captain of Company D, 2nd Battalion of Georgia Cavalry (Company B of the Georgia Hussars). He attained the rank of major in 1864.

After the war, William Wiltberger operated the Pulaski House and fulfilled his father's desire to turn part of Bonaventure into a public cemetery. In June 1868, he formed the Evergreen Cemetery Company and was made its first president. John Stoddard was the first chairman. Major Wiltberger died in 1872 and was buried next to his family in Section B, lot 3 of the cemetery he helped create. (Photo taken April 1998.)

STATE OF GEORGIA.

This Indenture, made this *Tenth* day of *January* in year of our Lord Eighteen Hundred and *Fifty Seven* **Between WILLIAM H. WILTBERGER,** of the County of Chatham State of Georgia, of the first part, **and** *William B. Hodgson*

of *the County of Chatham and State of Georgia* of the second

Witnesseth, that the said **WILLIAM H. WILTBERGER,** for and in consideration of the sum of *One Hundred Dollars —* to him in hand well and truly paid by the said *William B. Hodgson*

at and before the sealing and delivery of these Presents, the receipt whereof is hereby acknowledged, **HATH** granted, bargained, s conveyed and confirmed, and by these Presents, **DOTH** grant, bargain, sell, convey and confirm unto the said *William B. Hodgson his* heirs and assigns, **all** *that* portion of ground, or **Burial Lot** in the Cemetery at Bonáventure, in the County of Chatham State of Georgia, called **"THE EVERGREEN CEMETERY OF BONAVENTURE,"** known and distinguished in the plan of said Cemetery as Lot number *Thirteen* Section *D*, containing *Twenty five* feet in length *Twenty four* feet in width.

This image shows an indenture between William B. Hodgson, the scholar and statesman for whom the Georgia Historical Society's Hodgson Hall was created, and William H. Wiltberger, for a burial lot at the Evergreen Cemetery of Bonaventure. The lot mentioned in this document is lot 13 of Section D and is described as 25 feet in length and 24 feet wide. This indenture was a standard form used by Wiltberger and the Evergreen Cemetery Company. It is dated January 10, 1857, and is part of the Jones Family Papers at the Georgia Historical Society. William B. Hodgson was buried in Section D of this cemetery, but not in lot 13. His grave is located in Section D, lot 19. The Jones family (Noble, Noble Wymberly, and George Wymberly) is located in lot 13 of Section D.

After William Wiltberger's death, all titles to Bonaventure and the cemetery tracts were transferred to the Evergreen Cemetery Company by the executors of his estate. The Evergreen Cemetery (or the Evergreen Cemetery of Bonaventure, as it was also known) was bought by the city of Savannah in July 1907 for $30,000. The cemetery is maintained by the city's Park and Tree Commission. These two images show different views of the cemetery's entrance. The top image is from a postcard. In the bottom image, one can see the old railroad crossing that used to run by the cemetery.

On December 1, 1860, this etching and the etching at the bottom of the next page appeared in a *Harpers Weekly* article on Bonaventure Cemetery. These are some of the earliest images of the cemetery. The above image is described as the "Entrance to Bonaventure Cemetery, Savannah, Georgia." The article quotes heavily from *Life and Liberty in America*, a travel book by Dr. Charles Mackay (published in London, 1859) of England. Mackay (1814–1889) was traveling on a lecture tour throughout the United States from 1857 to 1858 when he visited Georgia in the early spring of 1858. He was particularly impressed with Bonaventure's "mournful avenues of live oak" and stated that "Never was a place more beautifully adapted by nature for such an object." He compared the moss hanging from the trees to "the tattered banners hung from the roofs of Gothic cathedrals as trophies of war in the olden time."

This image comes from a stereograph, and it also shows the original entrance gates to Bonaventure. The date of it is not known, but it must date from the latter part of the 19th century. These rustic-looking gates are no longer standing. It is not known when these gates were replaced with the current stone pillars.

Very few graves inhabited the cemetery at the time of this etching. Even at this early date in the cemetery's history, the moss-covered trees presented an elegant backdrop for a burial ground. A small building can still be seen on the left, possibly a relic from Bonaventure's plantation days.

The top photograph, taken in 1908 by Richard Stratton of Philadelphia, is one of the earliest-dated images showing the current entrance gates. The gates greet thousands of visitors a year. It is not known when these gates were erected. The bottom image is from a postcard, the date of which is uncertain.

Bonaventure has long been famous for its serene beauty and garden-like atmosphere. This top image, dated 1875, is from a stereograph and shows some of the cemetery's old oak trees. It was probably taken by J.N. Wilson, a local Savannah photographer who worked around the end of the 19th century. The bottom photograph shows some of the many azaleas that brighten the cemetery's streets with their blaze of colors when they bloom each spring. Bonaventure has 27 miles of azaleas. This image was taken in 1936.

Shortly after being built, the main house at Bonaventure reportedly burned one evening during a dinner party being held by either Colonel John Mullryne or Josiah Tattnall Sr. The fire started in the roof, and by the time it was noticed, the house could not be saved. Rather than disrupt his guests, Bonaventure's host had the dining room table moved outdoors and dinner served in the garden. The party continued by the warm light of the burning house.

Bonaventure has always had many visitors, including photographers. This top image shows a photographer, his helper, and a tent which probably served as a portable darkroom. The same photographer appears with friends in the picture to the right. He is in the back on the right wearing the hat. Over the years, this photographer has been variously identified as local Savannah photographer J. N. Wilson and as nationally acclaimed Civil War photographer Matthew Brady.

As a Victorian-era cemetery, Bonaventure reflects the changing views on death and dying held by middle-class Victorian America. Death became more romanticized and ritualized during this time period. Cemeteries soon followed course, becoming lush and beautiful "cities of the dead"

where people wanted to travel. One author writes that because of Bonaventure's beauty, "Death is robbed of half its horrors."

Another early visitor wrote of Bonaventure that "This hallowed burial place is like a natural cathedral, whose columns are majestic trees; whose stained-glass is its gorgeous foliage; whose tapestries are draperies of long gray moss; whose pavement is the flowery turf; whose aisles are avenues of softened light and shade; whose monuments are these elaborate and tasteful marble shafts, which tell in simple lines the names of those who here repose in dreamless sleep." The top image is from a postcard and the bottom from a stereograph.

Many authors have been moved by Bonaventure's beauty. I.M. Marsh published a poem about Bonaventure in 1860 in Savannah. In his 21-page composition, he writes about how "Here man can calmly sleep the sleep of death; Fanned by the swaying breezes gentle breath, the dreamless sleep—the sleep eternal, laid Darkly shrouded beneath thy cooling shade."

Bonaventure Cemetery

According to the original bylaws, rules, and regulations of the Evergreen Cemetery Company, published in Savannah in 1870, the price of lots was fixed at 8 1/3¢ per square foot. Money received from the sale of lots was to be used for the care and upkeep of the cemetery. For an annual fee of $5 per 300-square foot lot, the Cemetery Company agreed to maintain the lot itself. Owners had the right to erect any kind or number of monuments, stones, or markers and to plant any kind of trees, shrubs, or plants. However, there were a few restrictions on lot owners with regards to the cemetery lots. If any of the trees or plants became detrimental to other lots or the main avenues, the managers of the cemetery had the right to come in and remove the intruding flora. Likewise, if any monument or statue was deemed offensive to the cemetery managers, it could be removed. Fences placed around lots had to have prior approval from the managers.

Another story about Bonaventure's allure states that a clergyman committed suicide in the cemetery in the hopes of being buried there. This story appears in an 1858 letter to the *New Orleans Picayune* from a woman named Belle Brittan. Brittan writes that she heard this story "a few years ago" about a clergyman who "was smitten with the beauty of death" and plunged into the Wilmington River. This letter was published about a hundred years later in the *Savannah Morning News*.

In October of 1867, naturalist John Muir walked 1,000 miles from Louisville, Kentucky to the Florida Keys. He spent five days and nights camping in Bonaventure Cemetery while awaiting a package of money to be delivered to him. He described Bonaventure in his notes, which were published posthumously in 1916. He notes screaming bald eagles, which are no longer found there roosting among the trees, and the magnificent avenue of live oak trees, which still exists. With all the activities of the birds and insects, he commented, quite ironically, that Bonaventure seemed full of life. Muir later went on to found the Sierra Club, an environmental and wilderness conservation group, in 1892.

Henry Rootes Jackson, who is buried in the cemetery, wrote a poem about Bonaventure that was published in the November 1842 issue of *Orion Monthly Magazine*. Entitled "Buonaventure, by Starlight," Jackson writes of walking along a tree-lined corridor "where, like a tapestry o'er head, the gray moss floats upon the breeze." In a footnote to this poem, the magazine editor writes of "Tatnall's solitary tomb" and wonders why this place should not become a cemetery. He states that "hundreds of similar monuments would harmonize sweetly with the silent and almost thrilling grandeur of the place." Only a few years later, this editor's wish would become reality.

Bonaventure may seem timeless, but it continues to undergo change. In 1942, the city of Savannah began imposing restrictions on cemetery plots at Bonaventure to simplify maintenance of the cemetery. For lots bought after 1942, no planting is allowed and only one upright monument is allowed per lot. Other markers may be erected in the lot, but they must be level with the ground. Lots purchased prior to 1942 do not come under these new restrictions.

One of the earliest accounts about Bonaventure Cemetery's beauty comes from an anonymous letter published in the *Savannah Daily Republican* on July 25, 1849, shortly after Peter Wiltberger bought the property from Commodore Tattnall. The author, who identifies himself only as "A Stranger," observes on his visit to Bonaventure that "active preparations are going on to fit this place for a cemetery" and mentions seeing the Tattnall family graves. The visitor also states that Peter Wiltberger's plans for Bonaventure include "a neat chapel and a spacious receiving vault," neither of which have ever been erected.

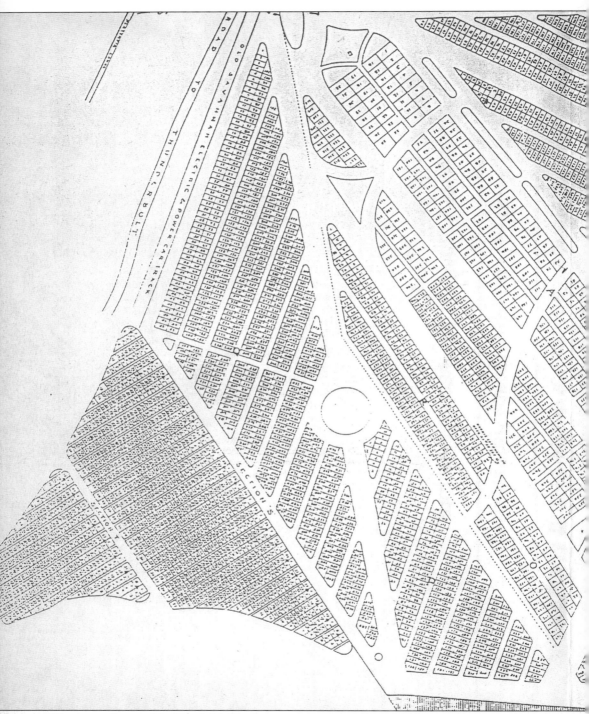

This map, designed by Frank M. Donlevy, gives an overall view of Bonaventure's layout. The map was adopted by the Park and Tree Commission in 1908, shortly after the city took control of the cemetery, and was revised in 1957. The large oval on the right side is Section F, where it

is thought Bonaventure's plantation house once stood. St. Augustine's Creek (Wilmington River), which the cemetery overlooks, is on the right. The cemetery's entrance is in the upper left.

In many ways, Bonaventure is more like a sculpture garden than a cemetery. Bonaventure was created during a time in the 19th century when people designed cemeteries not to just house the dead, but to be enjoyed by the living. These cemeteries were forerunners to modern public parks. Families then also had a much closer tie to cemeteries. They would visit their family plot often and were responsible for its maintenance and upkeep.

The strong live oak trees of Bonaventure are particularly well suited for Savannah's semi-tropical climate. They are strong enough to withstand hurricane force winds, resist rot, and are highly resistant to salt spray. The Spanish moss that hangs from the trees of Bonaventure has been catching people's attention for over 200 years. This airborne plant is not harmful to the trees like a parasite is; instead, it draws its nutrients from the air. However enchanting the moss may seem, though, it is definitely better to look and not touch when it comes to this plant. Spanish moss contains tiny red bugs, known as chiggers, that can be extremely irritating to humans and other vertebrates.

Age has not lessened Bonaventure's beauty or its appeal to visitors. Eva J. Barrington wrote in a 1950 article in the *Savannah Morning News* that "Bonaventure today, after nearly two centuries, is more beautiful than ever for the oaks have grown until they overlap forming cloistered aisles resembling a great outdoor Cathedral veiled with curtains of *tillandsia* (Spanish moss) gently swaying in the breeze creating an atmosphere of natural mourning." She also goes on to state that at Bonaventure "one does not experience the sadness and loneliness usually associated with such places but rather a sense of peace and repose."

Two

GREENWICH

"Say, have you lived within Savannah's bounds
And heard not of 'Old Greenwich Home' and grounds?

That tangled mass of briers and weeds
Where thistle and night-shade drop their seeds.
Was once a garden of flowers rare . . . "

These excerpts are from the poem, "On Old Greenwich," written by Elizabeth Ann Bowen Beecroft, who grew up at Greenwich Plantation more than 200 years ago. The photograph is from the early part of the 20th century.

During the Revolutionary War, the Siege of Savannah occurred in September and October, 1779. Greenwich Plantation, home of the Samuel Bowen family, became the headquarters for the French officers. The battle for Savannah took place on October 9. During this battle, 377 men were wounded, including Count Casimir Pulaski (left). A Polish noble who joined the American Revolution, Pulaski became a local hero.

Mystery shrouds the details of Pulaski's death and burial. Some stories say that once wounded, he was taken aboard the American warship *Wasp* where he died and was buried at sea. Others say that he died on the ship, but was buried on St. Helena's Island, South Carolina. Another version is that Pulaski was taken to Greenwich with the rest of the wounded men, died, and was buried there. Many of the other wounded probably died at Greenwich and are buried in unknown graves at Bonaventure and Greenwich.

The ownership history of Greenwich Plantation is rather murky. The plantation was bought from the Bowens in 1797 by Dr. Samuel Beecroft. Dr. Beecroft married the Bowens's daughter Elizabeth Ann. The land was later divided amongst their children. Years later, in 1874, the Savannah Schutzen Gesellschaft—a German rifle club—purchased the land from Captain F.C. Threadcraft to turn into a park. To help cover the purchase cost of $8,600, they opened club membership to allow non-German Americans to join. The club built a number of buildings in their new Schutzen Platz, including a ballroom, a bowling alley, shooting house, and barroom. This photograph was taken by William Wilson between 1883 and 1892.

The Schutzen Gesellschaft had wonderful parties and festivals on the grounds of Greenwich. Shooting contests were held and German rifle clubs from other cities would travel to the park. The Savannah Schutzen Gesellschaft closed in 1887. That same year, the Greenwich Park Association was formed. The idea of George W. Owens, chairman, and the other stockholders, was to improve and beautify the property as a country club or park. The photograph here shows one of the buildings at Greenwich before 1897, perhaps built by the Schutzen Gesellschaft.

In 1897, Spencer P. Shotter purchased Greenwich. Shotter, who was chairman of American Naval Stores, had also been a director of the Greenwich Park Association. He commissioned Carriere and Hastings, architects from New York City who had designed the Metropolitan Opera House, to design the house pictured above. Built from brick and marble, the house had three stories and 40 rooms. It was reported to have cost Shotter $500,000 to build and $100,000 to furnish. The gold-leafed ballroom was said to have cost $40,000 alone.

Greenwich's house and grounds were the setting for some early motion pictures. *Under Southern Skies*, a film set in colonial times, was filmed at Greenwich around 1915. Some of the early movie stars who were filmed at Greenwich included Marguerite Clark, Beverly Bayne, Francis X. Bushman, and Mary Pickford. The undated photograph to the right is labeled "Scene—Mice and Men."

Many newspaper articles have been written about how beautiful and picturesque Greenwich was. In 1917, Dr. H.N. Torrey of Detroit bought Greenwich. An article written for the *Savannah Morning News* about the sale of Greenwich was carried by the Associated Press throughout the United States. Greenwich was said to have been one of the most magnificent private homes in the south, rivaled only by Biltmore in North Carolina. This picture of the porch is from a photograph album owned by Mrs. Eleanor Torrey West and housed at the Georgia Historical Society. Mrs. West is the daughter of Dr. Torrey.

Pictured above is the hall on the main floor. Located off the hall was the drawing room, morning room, Indian room, library, billiard room, cloak and hat room, and the dining room. At the end of the hall is the statue of Eve, considered second only to the Venus de Milo, and for which Mr. Shotter paid $25,000. Most of the furnishings were included in Dr. Torrey's purchase of Greenwich.

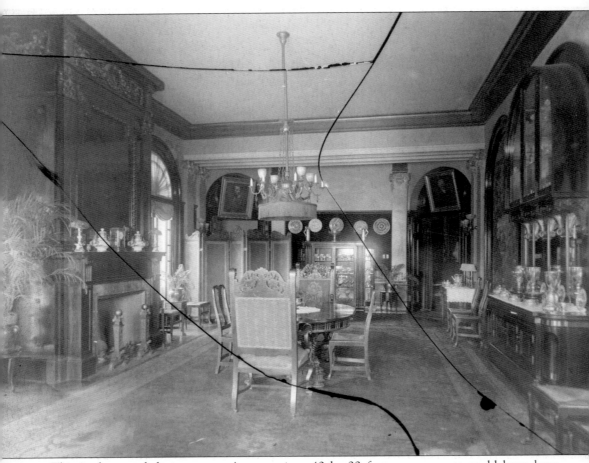

This is the grand dining room. At a spacious 40 by 22 feet, many guests could have been entertained here. The dining room was finished in solid mahogany. This photograph appears to have been printed from a broken glass plate negative, which would account for the black lines or cracks in the picture.

This image is the only other interior photograph of the Greenwich mansion. It appears to be the morning room. It has the cozy atmosphere of a family room, rather than the usual formality evident in drawing rooms. There are personal touches such as stacks of books and photographs. In January of 1923, fire destroyed the main house at Greenwich. Although no one was hurt, Eleanor Torrey and her nurse had to jump from a second-story window. Greenwich was never rebuilt.

Not only was the main house magnificent, the grounds were just as grand. This picture, from Mrs. West's album, shows some of the other buildings on the grounds of Greenwich. The 1917 newspaper article lists a garage that could accommodate six cars, a laundry facility, a superintendent's office and cottage, a lodge at the gates, a cottage for chauffeurs, and quarters for other servants. There was also an artificial pond behind the house.

Pictured above is another building on the grounds of Greenwich. The area surrounding the main house and gardens contained about 15 acres. When the Torrey family bought the property, the total size of Greenwich was approximately 100 acres. Besides the numerous outbuildings, there was also a dairy farm for the residents of Greenwich. After the 1923 fire, the Torrey family sold Greenwich. The property changed hands several times before the city of Savannah purchased it in 1937.

Located near the river, this building housed an indoor swimming pool. The photograph on this page is from Mrs. West's photo album and shows the pool house in its glory days. The interior was covered in green and white tile and the pool was approximately 20 by 30 feet. When the city of Savannah purchased Greenwich, one proposal was to convert the pool house into a temporary chapel.

The photographs seen here were taken in 1958 and show the obvious deterioration of the pool house. The picture above is an interior view, looking down into the bottom of the pool. Below, the general unkempt appearance of the pool house and grounds is apparent. The pool house is no longer standing.

This picturesque bridge was also on the grounds of Greenwich. Because of the open space to the left of the bridge, it appears to have been located near the river or marsh area. It may have been near the pool house, leading to the dock. The original photograph is from Mrs. West's photo album.

Above are the current entrance gates to Greenwich, as they appeared in April 1998. The approach, according to the 1917 newspaper article, was approximately three quarters of a mile long. The well-trimmed bushes that lined the drive are evident in the postcard below.

The gardens at Greenwich were as famous as the house. Mr. Shotter filled the gardens and grounds with imported plants and trees, as well as antiquities. As in all other aspects of building his home at Greenwich, Mr. Shotter apparently spared no expense in furnishing statuary for his garden. The two statues on either side of the ellipse are Janus figures.

Two sphinxes stood guard at the entrance to the formal gardens. Each was 7 feet long and had been sculpted in Egypt in approximately 300 B.C. The photograph above is from *c*. 1935. The photograph below is undated.

After the 1923 fire and the Torrey's departure, the sculpture remained in the gardens at Greenwich. The statuary was so famous that Al Capone, while imprisoned at Alcatraz, tried to purchase the collection. When the city bought the land in 1937 and decided to use it as a cemetery, the busts and statues were removed. For 30 years the statues were stored at Laurel Grove Cemetery.

In 1965, according to a newspaper article, the Telfair Academy of Arts and Sciences requested that the statuary be placed under their care. The statues were restored and some of the smaller pieces were placed on display. One third century bust, that of Emperor Caracalla, who ruled from 211–217 B.C., went to the Owens-Thomas House.

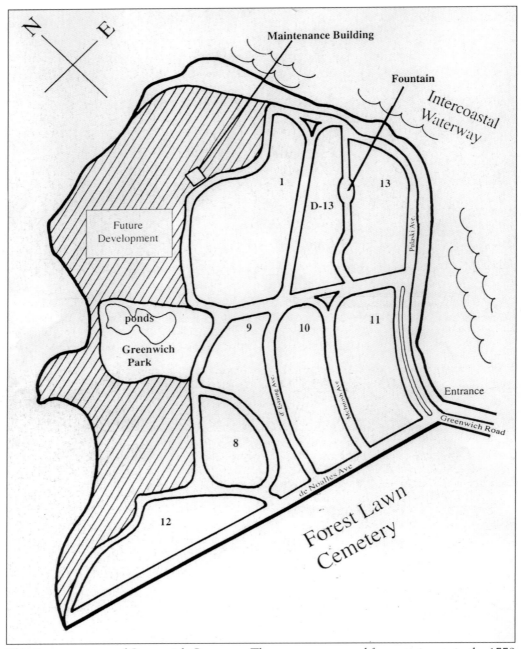

This is a recent map of Greenwich Cemetery. The streets are named for participants in the 1779 Battle of Savannah: d'Estaing, McIntosh, Pulaski, and de Noalles Avenues.

A 1943 newspaper article states that the city designated Greenwich Cemetery as the "Greenwich Addition to Bonaventure Cemetery." Plots, which were available that same year, came under modern regulations. No curbs, hedges, plants, or trees were permitted in or around the plot. Only one marker of marble or granite could be erected. Below, this photograph shows what is left of the artificial pond, an area where there are no burial lots. (Photos taken April 1998.)

The postcard above illustrates the beauty of the artificial pond. The caption reads: "Greenwich . . . Showing weeping willow, which formerly overhung the grave of Napoleon Bonaparte at St. Helena." The postcard was made during the time that Dr. Torrey owned Greenwich, sometime between 1917 and 1923. Pictured below is the only extant part of the bridge, the lower portions of the brick supports. The bridge crossed at a narrow neck in the middle of two free-formed sections. (Photo taken April 1998.)

The pond was originally 1.5 acres in size and resembled a butterfly. The northern portion of the pond has retained its shape. However, the section south of the bridge has lost much of its definition over the years. Its edges have been choked by weeds and trees. The weeping willow tree (seen on the top of the previous page) has also disappeared. The photograph above was taken looking south, towards the cemetery. The narrow area where the bridge stood is visible. The photo below looks towards the north. In this image, the cement retaining wall at the back of the pond is evident. (Photos taken April 1998.)

This fountain serves as a reminder of Greenwich's past as well as its present. It is the original fountain that was placed in front of the main house in 1898. The fountain was created by William Roche of Roche Stone and Monument Company, located in Savannah. In 1967, it was restored by Harben Daniel in memory of four family members who were killed in a car accident. They are buried nearby. Besides the pond, the fountain is the only remnant of the former glory of Greenwich Plantation. (Photos taken April 1998.)

Greenwich Plantation was created by combining a number of farm lots which were grants from King George II of England. This fountain was placed here in 1898. It was restored in 1967 by Harben Daniel in loving memory of

CATHERINE MURREY DANIEL
CATHERINE DANIEL LONG
CHRISTOPHER DANIEL LONG
ROBERT BRINKER LONG, JR.

Three
IN SILENT SLUMBER

The appeal of Bonaventure's idyllic beauty transcends time. Since 1846, many people of diverse backgrounds have been laid to rest under the live oak trees. Military generals and children, people of world renown and the general public—they are all buried here. In Bonaventure's early days, even colonial citizens were moved from their original burial sites to the newly formed cemetery. Pictured here is the 20th-century stone of Henry Frederick Grimm (1858–1933) and Catherine Meta Grimm (1865–1910). This photograph was taken in 1946.

In 1754, William Butler (1715–1761) was granted lots in George Town, Georgia. He was appointed tax collector and surveyor of highways. In 1755 he established Silk Hope Plantation; in 1759 he was appointed to the council. His gravestone eulogizes his "Amiable Qualities" and "Benevolent Disposition." William Butler's grave is believed to be the oldest in Bonaventure. However, it is not original to the site. (Section F, lot 50. Photo taken July 1998.)

E.A. Martin Schroder (1854–1927) and his wife Minna (1857–1937) were both natives of Germany. After immigrating to Savannah, he eventually became an alderman and a director of the National Bank of Savannah, the Oglethorpe Savings and Trust Company, and the Mutual Fire Insurance Company of Savannah. The Schroders' tomb is located at Section C, lot 15.

Duncan Lamont Clinch (1784–1849), a U.S. Army officer, became a brigadier general in 1829. He commanded at the Battle of Ouithlacoochee against the Seminoles in 1835. In 1844 he was elected to fill a vacancy as a U.S. Representative; he served until 1845. The Clinch tomb sits at Section C, lot 16.

The Mongin-Stoddard tomb is dedicated to John David Mongin (1760–1833). Mongin owned land on Daufuskie Island and also owned one of the first steamboats to operate between Savannah and Charleston. The vault, which held ten family members, was moved from Daufuskie to Bonaventure in 1873. In 1989, the tomb was vandalized. The door was broken, and most of the bones were stolen. (Section H, lot 99. Photo taken April 1998.)

Noble Jones (1702–1775), to the left, arrived with General Oglethorpe in 1733. He was a physician and carpenter and became the first colonial surveyor. In 1756, he was granted land and founded Wormsloe Plantation. Tabby ruins of the fortress he built are still extant. Noble Jones's grave, below, is located in Section D, lot 13. (Taken April 1998.) To the near right is Jones's grandson, George Wymberly Jones (1766–1838). This image is a photograph taken of the portrait painted by Rembrandt Peale. Jones was a doctor like his father and grandfather. After inheriting Wormsloe, he began work on the current house. Jones was appointed Georgia Superior Court Judge in 1804 and to the U.S. Senate in 1807. On the far right is the Jones Monument, which was erected in 1848 and dedicated to George W. Jones and his daughter Letitia.

George Wymberly Jones De Renne (1827–1880), the son of George Wymberly Jones, added the maternal family name of De Renne. He was a great collector of Georgia historical material. He moved the graves of his father and colonial ancestors to Bonaventure. His grave, seen below, is also located in Section D, lot 13. (Taken April 1998.)

Mary Telfair (1791–1875) was the daughter of Edward (1735–1807) and Sarah Gibbons Telfair (1758–1827). The Telfairs were an eminent Georgia family. Mary Telfair was one of three daughters; she never married. She inherited her family's Savannah home, which had been designed by William Jay. In turn, she bequeathed the house to become the Telfair Academy of Arts and Sciences. Mary also founded the Telfair Hospital for Females and the Telfair Home for Widows. The original of this portrait hangs at the Telfair Academy of Arts and Sciences.

IN MEMORY OF
SARAH TELFAIR, WIDOW OF EDWARD TELFAIR
AND OF THEIR DAUGHTERS
SARAH G. HAIG, WIDOW OF CAPT. GEORGE HAIG, U.S.A.
MARGARET T. HODGSON, WIDOW OF WILLIAM B. HODGSON
MARY TELFAIR

The Telfair men were active in Georgia politics. Edward was a delegate to the 1778 Continental Congress. He became governor of Georgia in 1786. One son, Thomas, was elected to the Georgia Legislature. There he helped draft the first criminal code adopted anywhere in the United States. He was a U.S. Representative from 1813 to 1817. Another son, Alexander, was a prominent Savannah merchant. This monument is placed in the memory of Sarah Gibbons Telfair and Edward Telfair and their daughters and sons: Sarah Haig, Margaret Hodgson, Mary Telfair (pictured on facing page), Edward, Thomas, Josiah G., and Alexander. The monument was erected in 1860 by Margaret and Mary. This image shows the side of the monument listing the mother and daughters. The monument is located in Section D, lot 19. (Photo taken April 1998.)

William Brown Hodgson (1801–1871) was an important figure in the early history of the Georgia Historical Society. The Society was founded in 1839 and Hodgson became the first curator in 1845, filling that role until 1870. Prior to his involvement with the Society, Hodgson was the U.S. Consul in Algiers 1826–1829. This portrait, painted by Carl Brandt, hangs in the library of the Georgia Historical Society.

WILLIAM B. HODGSON
A NATIVE OF VIRGINIA
FOR NEARLY TWENTY NINE YEARS
A RESIDENT OF SAVANNAH
DIED IN THE CITY OF NEW YORK
26TH JUNE A. D. 1871
HIS REMAINS REPOSE IN THE ADJACENT VAULT

THIS MONUMENT
IS ERECTED BY A BEREAVED WIFE
TO THE MEMORY OF HER BELOVED
HUSBAND

After Hodgson's death, his wife, Margaret Telfair Hodgson, had the Georgia Historical Society's headquarters built as a memorial to him. Completed in 1875, it is known as Hodgson Hall. Margaret Hodgson also erected this monument at Bonaventure. The epitaph reads, in part: "This monument is erected by a bereaved wife to the memory of her beloved husband." This monument is located at Section D, lot 19. (Photo taken April 1998.)

Richard Dennis Arnold (1808–1876) was a distinguished Savannah physician. He helped to found the American Medical Association, the Medical Association of Georgia, and the now defunct Savannah Medical College. Arnold was also a founder of the Georgia Historical Society. He was mayor of Savannah from 1842 to 1865. As the mayor in 1864, he surrendered the city of Savannah to General Sherman. The portrait (top) was painted by Emma Cheeves Wilkins. Arnold's monument (left) stands in Section F, lot 34. (Photo of grave taken April 1998.)

Judge Peter Wiltberger Meldrim (1848–1933) was born in Savannah and received a law degree from the University of Georgia in 1869. He then began practicing law in Savannah. He served in both houses of the Georgia State Legislature. In 1917, he was appointed Judge of the Eastern Judicial Circuit, a position he held until his death. This photograph was taken by W.W. Hoffman of Savannah.

Peter Meldrim married Frances Bird Casey in 1881. In 1892, he purchased the former home of Charles Green on Macon Street. Green's house was well known as the residence of William T. Sherman during the Union's occupation of Savannah. The Meldrim family lived in this home until 1943. Peter Meldrim is buried in Section H, lot 97. Some Meldrim family papers are at the Georgia Historical Society. (Photo taken July 1998.)

Brigadier General Alexander Robert Lawton (1818–1896) was born in the Beaufort district of South Carolina. He graduated from West Point in 1839 and received a law degree from Harvard in 1842. After finishing Harvard, he moved to Savannah and practiced law there until 1849. He was elected president of the Augusta and Savannah Railroad in 1850 and served in this capacity until 1854. He was then elected to the Georgia House of Representatives and served there from 1855 to 1856. In 1859, he was elected to a term in the state senate. At the outbreak of the Civil War, Lawton was made a brigadier general in the Confederate Army and eventually became quartermaster-general of the Confederacy. After the war, he resumed his law practice in Savannah. He was a member of the state legislature from 1870 to 1875 and was vice-president of the state constitutional convention in 1877. He served as president of the American Bar Association from 1882 to 1883, U.S. Minister to Austria from 1887 to 1889, and became the first president of the Savannah Bar Association in 1894.

LAWTON MONUMENT, BONAVENTURE CEMETERY, SAVANNAH, GA.

General Lawton married Sarah Hillhouse Alexander of Washington, Georgia on November 5, 1845. The couple had four children—three daughters and a son. Their eldest child, Corinne, was born in 1846. She died in 1877 and was originally buried in Laurel Grove Cemetery. Her father died in Clifton Springs, New York in 1896 and was also originally buried in Laurel Grove Cemetery. Both the father's and daughter's remains were removed to Bonaventure on April 26, 1898. They are both buried in Section H, lots 166–167. The large arched monument on the right, sculpted by Professor R. Romanellit in Florence, Italy in 1898, honors General Lawton's memory. The statue in front of the arch depicts Jesus. The monument in the foreground of a woman seated in front of a cross memorializes Corinne Lawton. These beautiful monuments have been well photographed and are often used to represent the cemetery. This image comes from a postcard.

Henry Rootes Jackson (1820–1898), a lawyer, soldier, statesman, and writer, was born in Athens, Georgia. He graduated from Yale in 1839 and began practicing law in Savannah. From 1846 to 1847, he served as colonel of the 1st Georgia Regiment in the Mexican War. In 1849, he was appointed judge of the Superior Court of Georgia, where he served until 1853. In 1850, he published his first book of poetry and became known as a Southern poet. He served as U.S. minister to Austria from 1853 to 1858. He was commissioned as brigadier general in the Confederate Army in 1861. He was captured at Nashville and held prisoner until the end of the war. After the war, he resumed his legal practice in Savannah. In 1867, he was appointed minister to Mexico. This photograph is of a portrait of Jackson that was done by Carl L. Brandt.

Henry Rootes JACKSON Monument.

BONAVENTURE CEMETERY.

Lawton Monument

From 1875 until his death, General Jackson was president of the Georgia Historical Society. He was the first president of the Telfair Academy of Arts and Sciences. In 1892, he became president of Central Railroad and Banking, a position he held until his death at age 77. Jackson was twice married. His first wife was Cornelia Augusta Davenport of Savannah. His second wife was Florence Barclay King of St. Simons Island. Jackson died in Savannah and is buried in Section H, lot 101, next to his second wife. Florence Jackson died August 28, 1912, at the age of 78. This photograph of his grave site was taken c. 1925. Jackson's grave is located not far from General Lawton's grave. Some of Henry R. Jackson's papers are located at the Georgia Historical Society.

Robert Houstoun Anderson (1835–1888) was born in Savannah. He graduated from West Point in 1857 and served in the United States Army after graduation. He resigned from the U.S. Army and accepted a commission from the Confederacy in 1861, eventually attaining the rank of brigadier general. He served in the Confederate Army until the South's surrender in 1865. The image of Anderson (left) is from the Society's print collection. The monument below (photographed April 1998) marks the grave of Captain Robert H. Anderson (1861–1901), the son of General Anderson. Captain Anderson was serving in the 9th U.S. Infantry in the Philippines when he, like his father, died of pneumonia.

After the war, General Anderson became chief of the Savannah police, a position he held from 1866 until 1888. As police chief, Anderson helped shape Savannah's forces into a well-organized unit. He also organized and served as president of the Savannah Sabre Club after the war. He died in Savannah and is buried in Section F, lot 12. Near his grave is a monument that was "Erected in memory of their Chief by the Police Force of Savannah along with contributions from members of the Georgia Hussars Rifle Association, Knights Templar, Hibernian Society and other friends." A bust of Anderson sits atop this monument. His wife, Sarah Clitz Anderson, is buried beside him. She died on October 18, 1906, at age 71. Her grave is marked by the white marble wreath. (Photo taken July 1998.)

Solomon Wilson Gleason (1821–1876) was a prominent Savannah machinist. His only son died in 1869 and his wife in 1875. They were buried in the family plot at Bonaventure. In Gleason's diary, which is now at the Georgia Historical Society, he talks about going to Bonaventure to visit his beloved son and wife. Gleason died in Savannah's 1876 yellow fever epidemic. (Photo taken April 1998.)

Dr. Brodie S. Herndon (1810–1886) came to Savannah from Fredericksburg, Virginia. He served in the Confederate Army as chief surgeon of hospitals in Richmond, Virginia. He was the first person to perform a Cesarean operation in the United States. Dr. Herndon's remains were removed from Fernandina to Bonaventure in 1878. He is buried in Section F, lot 19, next to his wife Lucy (1813–1880). (Photo taken April 1998.)

Dr. Phineas Miller Kollock (1804–1872), the son of Dr. Lemuel Kollock, was a doctor of obstetrics and diseases of women and children. During his career, he served as president and vice-president of the Georgia Medical Society and as a professor at the Savannah Medical College. Upon his death, his body was stored temporarily in a vault in Laurel Grove Cemetery. His remains were removed to Bonaventure Cemetery on March 5, 1878. He is buried in Section E, lot 2, along with other members of the Kollock family.

Beneath Bonaventure's shady oaks are buried veterans from almost every war in which the United States has been involved. The grave sites of veterans are designated by markers that were placed there by veterans' groups. This top photograph shows what the metal crosses honoring Confederate veterans look like. Many veterans are buried near each other. Members of Company A of the Georgia Hussars that served the Confederacy are buried in Section A, plot 116. Veterans from Worth Bagley Camp #10 that served in the Spanish-American War are buried in Section K, lots 41–42 and 59–60. Spanish-American War veterans' graves are signified by a metal cross like the one below. (Photos taken April 1998.)

Veterans from both World Wars are buried in the American Legion Field at Bonaventure. These two images show different views of the field. The entrance gates to the section bear a plaque that states that this field honors the memory of World War veterans from three local chapters of the American Legion. These chapters are Chatham Post 36, Savannah Post 135, and Tybee Island Post 154. (Photos taken April 1998.)

John Holbrook Estill (1840–1907) was born in Charleston, South Carolina. His family moved to Savannah in 1851. During the Civil War, Estill served as member of the Oglethorpe Light Infantry until he was discharged after being wounded at the First Battle of Manassas. A self-made newspaperman, Estill owned the *Savannah Morning News* from 1868 until his death.

Estill was a successful businessman, a member of the Georgia Historical Society, first president and a director of the Savannah Benevolent Association, and president of Bethesda Orphanage. He served 12 years as a county commissioner and 22 years on the board of education. He was also president of the Evergreen Cemetery Company from 1880 to 1907. This obelisk marks his grave. (Photo taken April 1998.)

John Herndon Mercer (1909–1976), better known as "Johnny" Mercer, was one of the most popular lyricists of the 20th century. He wrote over 1,500 songs and won four Academy Awards for his work. Born in Savannah, he grew up with his family on the island of Vernon View. His ashes are buried in Section H, lot 48 next to the remains of his wife, Elizabeth "Ginger." (Photo taken April 1998.)

Conrad Potter Aiken (1889–1973), the poet and writer, was born in Savannah. He graduated from Harvard in 1912 and wrote over 50 works in his life, including collections of poetry, stories, novels, criticisms, a fictionalized autobiographical memoir, and a play. He won a Pulitzer Prize in 1930. He died in Savannah and is buried in Section H, lot 78. His grave is marked by a marble bench. (Photo taken April 1998.)

This statue in Section A, lot 184, marks the graves of the two wives of Francis Joseph Ruckert. Ruckert's first wife was Barbara; the date of her death is unknown. Francis and Barbara were immigrants from Darmstadt, Germany. In the 1860 Federal Census for Georgia, Ruckert is listed as a liquor merchant. The 1870 census states that he was a saloon keeper. In the 1880s, the Savannah City Directory stated that Ruckert ran a saloon and restaurant on Broughton Street. After Barbara's death, Ruckert married Louisa, a native of Georgia, who died in Savannah on June 12, 1893, at the age of 54. (Photos taken April 1998.)

One of the first Greeks to immigrate to Savannah was a man named Eli Veruki. He arrived in Savannah in 1880. By 1911, the Greek community had close to 30 families. John P. Rousakis, the son of a Greek immigrant, was mayor of Savannah from 1970 to 1991. These photographs, showing the Greek area at Bonaventure, were taken in Section K in April 1998.

In 1907, Savannah's first Greek Orthodox parish was chartered. They soon outgrew their first church, and in 1941 Lawton Hall was purchased. Located at the corner of Bull and Anderson Streets, it was built originally as a memorial for A.R. Lawton and his daughter Corinne. Stained-glass panels and a dome were added before the church, St. Paul's Greek Orthodox Church, was dedicated in 1943.

In 1888, members of Congregation Mickve Israel first proposed the idea of purchasing land adjoining Bonaventure for the site of a new Jewish cemetery. Space in Laurel Grove Cemetery was growing more limited and new options had to be pursued. Initial plans fell through and it was not until the city of Savannah became custodian of Bonaventure that negotiations for a Jewish section began again. In 1909, plans were completed, and the new Jewish cemetery became a reality. It consisted of about 15 acres of land. Both Congregation Mickve Israel and Congregation B'nai B'rith Jacob were involved in the sale. This archway marks the entrance to the Jewish section at Bonaventure. (Photo taken April 1998.)

Following a funeral, Jews observe a formal period of mourning that lasts seven days and is known as *Shiva*. On the one-year anniversary of the funeral, the final mourning ritual, *Yahrzeit* (a Yiddish term for anniversary), is observed. On Yahrzeit, a small stone, similar to this one on the Udinsky/Benzel grave, is often left on the tombstone as a token of remembrance. (Photo taken April 1998.)

Jewish graves often have phrases carved in Hebrew on them. Carved atop this statue is an open copy of the Torah. This statue, in Section P, lot 66, commemorates the memory of Mrs. Rose Kass, the wife of Charles Kass. She died on November 10, 1918, at the age of 26. Mrs. Kass was not from Savannah, but was from Norman Park in Colquitt County, Georgia. (Photo taken April 1998.)

This Jewish chapel, located in Section Q, was built in 1917 by Hesed Shel Emeth (a female burial society). They purchased lots for the chapel from the city and had it built from private contributions. Originally, the chapel was used for Jewish burial rites. The chapel was vandalized in the 1970s, but was restored by members of the same burial society that had originally built it. It has approximately 780 square feet of space and is still used for memorial services. (Photos taken April 1998.)

פ"נ
ר' יצחק ב"ר צבי
נפטר א' אדר התש"א
ת'נ'צ'ב'ה

BELOVED HUSBAND
ISAAC
LITMAN
DIED FEB. 27, 1941
AGE 78 YEARS

DEVOTED FATHER

An interesting feature of tombstones in Bonaventure Cemetery is the inclusion of photographs of the deceased. These images are set in a frame in the stone and are prevalent in the Jewish section of Bonaventure. Most of them are in remarkably good condition. Isaac Litman ran a wholesale leather store in Savannah for several years under the name I. Litman and Sons. He died on February 27, 1941, at the age of 78. Litman had three daughters and five sons. (Photo taken April 1998.)

The Gaston Vault (also known as the Stranger's Vault) sits at the entrance of Bonaventure Cemetery. It was originally erected in the entrance of Colonial Cemetery, but was removed to Bonaventure in 1873. This marble tomb was built as a memorial to William Gaston, who died in New York City in 1837. A respected Savannah merchant, Gaston was well known for his hospitality and kindness to others, particularly strangers. Upon his death, Savannahians took up a subscription to build this unique memorial. It was designed as a temporary resting place for the bodies of strangers who died in Savannah. Eventually, Gaston's remains were brought South and re-interred in the tomb. During the Civil War, Yankee soldiers occupied Colonial Cemetery during their stay in Savannah and broke open the vault. Reportedly, they did not disturb Gaston's remains. Mayor Thomas Gamble remarked in 1925 that Gaston was "Savannah's host to the living and the dead." (Photo taken April 1998.)

Four
THE LEGACY

Bonaventure is an excellent example of a Victorian-era cemetery. With its eclectic tombstones and monuments and moss-covered oak trees, Bonaventure appears to be more of a garden than a cemetery. The sculptures in this cemetery represent a dying art form. This monument to Corinne E. Lawton was sculpted by Civiletti Palormo in 1879. It is located in Section H, lots 166–167. (Photo taken April 1998.)

One of the most recognized sculptors of monuments in Savannah is John Walz (1844–1922).
Born in Stuttgart, Germany, Walz moved to Philadelphia at the age of 13 to live with his
married sister after the death of their parents. He eventually went back to Europe to study art
and sculpture. Carl Brandt (1831–1905), the first director of the Telfair Academy (now the
Telfair Art Museum), placed an order with Walz's employer for the large statues that stand in
front of the museum. (Brandt is also buried at Bonaventure in Section H, lot 94.) Walz worked
on the statues and accompanied them to Savannah in 1886. He fell in love with the city,
opened his own studio, and never left. His work has been exhibited in museums and galleries
and won numerous prizes. In addition to carving statues and memorials for cemeteries, Walz
also designed numerous public monuments in Savannah. In 1907, at age 63, Walz married
Sarah Gilmore.

Fittingly, John Walz is buried in the cemetery he so helped to beautify. He is buried in the Gilmore/Walz lot in Section A, lot 331. Surprisingly, though, there is no headstone at Walz's grave. A recently erected wooden sign is the only indicator of the final resting place of this talented sculptor. (Photo taken April 1998.)

Walz was well known for his funerary monuments, and his work can be found in many of Savannah's cemeteries, such as Bonaventure, Laurel Grove, and Catholic Cemetery. Over 70 works by Walz have been found in Bonaventure alone. This tree stump monument marks the grave of J.A. Schafer and is located in Section A, lot 185. (Photo taken April 1998.)

The mark of sculptor John Walz is usually very easily identified. As seen at the bottom of the Herschbach tombstone in the top photograph, Walz signed his pieces "J. Walz Sculptor Sav." Walz designed this grave for Mr. and Mrs. Joseph Herschbach in 1907, according to a newspaper article. Mrs. Bertha Dixon, one of the couple's four children, asked Walz to design the monument for her parents. The bottom photograph shows the footstone of the grave. A laurel branch adorns the shield. (Photos taken April 1998.)

Like John Walz, Joseph Herschbach (1822–1906) and his wife, Clara Goebel Herschbach (1830–1905), were natives of Germany. Perhaps they knew Walz personally through one of the many German societies in Savannah. Herschbach was in the cigar-manufacturing business and at one time had the largest cigar-manufacturing house in the city. Walz designed the grave in the Grecian style of architecture, with Ionic columns flanking the graceful angel in the center. The grave is bounded by marble on all sides. Herschbach was a Confederate veteran, as indicated by the CSA marker at the base of the tombstone. A 1907 article in the *Savannah Morning News* describes the grave as such: "The angel is carved in repose, with bowed head and a divine expression, to which the clouds and architecture as a background add harmoniously." The Herschbach's double grave is located in Section D, lots 32–33. The couple's only son, Julius A. Herschbach (1856–1921), is also buried in this lot. (Photo taken April 1998.)

One of Walz's most famous statues is the statue of little Gracie Watson (1883–1889), resting alone in Section E, lot 99. Gracie was the only child of W.J. and Frances Watson. Mr. Watson managed the Pulaski House, a famed Savannah hotel. According to an article in the *Savannah Morning News*, his daughter was known for her sweetness and was a favorite of hotel guests.

She contracted pneumonia and died two days after Easter in 1889. Her funeral was held in the parlors of the Pulaski House. The next year, the Watsons left Pulaski House and became managers of the newly opened DeSoto Hotel.

In 1890, Gracie's father went to see sculptor John Walz. According to legend, Watson took his only photograph of his beloved daughter and handed it to Walz, unable to speak. With his chisel and a block of white Georgia marble, Walz carved out a painstakingly detailed and chillingly life-like image of the child. Gracie's statue stands alone, marking the young child's grave. Her parents stayed at the DeSoto for many years, but eventually left Savannah. The child is the only person buried in the cemetery lot. Gracie's statue is a popular stop for visitors to Bonaventure, especially for children. Her appeal lies in her realism and the soft, serene vision on the child's face. Gifts are often left at her feet, such as shiny pennies or small presents at Christmas time.

John Walz was not the only person creating sculptures for Bonaventure. Another common sculptor's name on monuments at Bonaventure is Struthers of Philadelphia. Struthers sculpted this neo-Gothic monument for the grave of Edward and Elizabeth Padelford. Edward Padelford (1799–1870) was a prominent merchant who came to Savannah around 1820 from Massachusetts. He was a founder of St. John's Episcopal Church. According to a newspaper article, Padelford was very interested in the arts, and his funerary monument certainly reflects this interest. (Photos taken April 1998.)

Struthers's mark can be seen here at the foot of another of his creations, the monument to William Brown Hodgson in Section D, lot 19. (Photo taken April 1998.)

Struthers was not the only Northerner creating monuments for Bonaventure. W.F. Pietch of New York designed this memorial to John Stoddard. Stoddard (1809–1879) was very connected with Bonaventure's development as a cemetery, as he was the first chairman of the Evergreen Cemetery Company in 1868. He was also president of the Georgia Historical Society from 1867 to 1868. He is buried in Section C, lot 24. (Photo taken April 1998.)

Antonio Aliffi (1888–1936) was another fine Savannah sculptor. Born in Sicily, Aliffi came from a long line of Italian sculptors. He was invited to Savannah by none other than John Walz. Walz owned a marble yard and wanted Aliffi to carve for him. Aliffi was a very busy sculptor, working on projects in Savannah and around the country. He is reported to have carved on Georgia's Stone Mountain and Mount Rushmore in South Dakota, as well as on the ceiling of Savannah's Lucas Theatre. Unfortunately, locating Aliffi's great body of work is not easy, because very little of his work bears his mark. He may have even signed his employer's name to some of his work, a common practice at the time. The Orsini monument at Bonaventure has been attributed to Aliffi. Aliffi never made a lot of money as a sculptor. He was devastated with the crash of 1929 and went to work for Milton J. Little's Oglethorpe Monument Company. Aliffi died at the age of 48, leaving his wife Carmela to care for their nine children. (Photo taken April 1998.)

Like Aliffi, Sebastian Orsini (1873–1918) was also an Italian immigrant. He came to Savannah around 1898 and along with several brothers was involved in the grocery business. From 1912 to 1915, the Savannah City Directory listed him as proprietor of the Savannah Macaroni Works. Orsini's wife, Salvatrice, survived her husband by only a few months. The couple is buried in Section K, lot 376. (Photo taken April 1998.)

In 1920, Aliffi bought his own marble yard at the corner of Thirty-first and Paulsen Streets. This page from the 1921 Savannah City Directory lists Aliffi's (misspelled as Oliffi) yard at 1417 Vine Street. John Walz's marble yard and Little's Oglethorpe Monument Company are also listed. Aliffi sold his yard in 1924.

MONUMENTS
Manufacturers Since 1907

OGLETHORPE
MARBLE AND GRANITE CO.
PLANT AND DISPLAY

918 East Broad   **Telephone 232-5571**

The Oglethorpe Marble and Granite Company has been in the monument business since 1907, and many of the markers at Bonaventure came from this company. This advertisement (top) is from a 1963–1964 Savannah City Directory. The Celtic Cross icon used in the advertisement looks very similar to W.S. Chisolm's grave in Bonaventure (bottom photo taken April 1998). Chisolm (1836–1890) was a lawyer. The Oglethorpe Marble and Granite Company is still in existence today.

The variety of grave markers at Bonaventure is endless. They span from headstones to monuments and statues to functional pieces, such as the bench at the grave of Charles Graham (below). The epitaph for William Eugene (top left) reads: "Weep not for the sweetest bud that is missing for it fell asleep only to wake more bright and beautiful in the arms of Jesus." (Photos taken April 1998.)

Gravestones in Victorian-era cemeteries became more elaborate and beautiful than their Colonial-era counterparts. More hopeful images such as angels and cherubs replaced darker images such as skulls on tombs. These cherubs adorn the Dieter family monument in Section H. (Photo taken April 1998.)

Lambs are often used on children's headstones, such as this one at the grave of Robert V. Nottingham Jr. (1887–1892). The lamb is full of Biblical symbolism, representing innocence, sacrifice, and resurrection. This grave is located in Section H, lot 70. (Photo taken April 1998.)

Colonial Cemetery, Savannah's oldest existing cemetery, closed to burials in the mid-1850s. Laurel Grove and Bonaventure Cemeteries were created to meet citizens' burial needs. Many people buried in Colonial Cemetery were moved to these newer cemeteries, probably because there was more space in Laurel Grove and Bonaventure. Thus, more loved ones could be buried near each other. One example of that is the grave of Ann Marion Johnston. (Photo taken April 1998.)

Fair Stranger whose feet have wandered to this land of silence, Contemplate this Stone. Near it is interred Dust which once a lovely Form inhabited by a Mind, Superior in Intelligence worth and Amiableness to most of her sex. as a Daughter, Sister & Friend as a Wife and Mother, few whom she left behind can boast so bright an example.

Ann Marion Johnston (1778–1817) was the wife of Colonel James Johnston Jr. (1769–1822) and the third child of Sir George and Lady Ann Houston, a prominent family in early Georgia. Ann, her husband, and her parents were originally buried in Colonial Cemetery, but were later re-interred in the Kollock family lot at Bonaventure. This four-sided monument was erected in Ann's memory and contains a touching epitaph. (Photo taken April 1998.)

Bonaventure has always had a certain charm. Even as early as 1834, the date of this image, it appealed to sightseers. The grave and monument in the center are those of the Tattnall family. The Savannah Volunteer Guards erected the monument as a memorial to their former captain, Edward Fenwick Tattnall, who died in 1832. The riders are identified (from left to right) as Miss Mary Telfair, Mr. J. Farley, and Miss Sarah H. Campbell (later Kollock). Although it is possible that they rode out to Bonaventure to visit the grave site, the depiction is much more pastoral. The scene seems to be one of pleasant leisure. It is perhaps the earliest illustration of Bonaventure visitors.

The blossoming Victorian era, with its ideas of cemeteries as parks, increased the amount of visitors to Bonaventure. People came to walk the grounds, visit loved ones, and even to picnic. The picture to the right, one half of a stereograph, shows two men with a picnic basket. They are sitting in the avenue in front of the Jones Monument.

The caption for this postcard describes the allure of Bonaventure. "A popular drive is to Bonaventure, a beautiful city of the dead, four miles from Savannah. The scenery of Bonaventure has long been renowned for its Arcadian beauty; for its broad avenues of live oaks draped with pendant gray moss."

Mailed in 1906, this postcard illustrates how popular Bonaventure was becoming at the time. The place for Sunday outings and tourists, as well as Savannahians, the peaceful beauty of Bonaventure was enticing. The fact that postcards were made and sold demonstrates the cemetery's role as a tourist attraction.

The enchantment of Bonaventure continues to grow. With the recent popularity of the book *Midnight in the Garden of Good and Evil* by John Berendt, Bonaventure Cemetery has gained an almost cult status. The people in this photograph were part of a walking tour in April 1998.

The rutted avenue visible in this early photograph gives testimony to the multitudes of visitors at Bonaventure each year. Although the shady lanes remained the same, the atmosphere at Bonaventure was changing.

As time progressed, so did the modes of transportation. Replacing horses and carriages, the early automobile shown in this postcard was probably still something of an oddity. This moss-draped lane is the main drive through Section A.

On a typical day, several cars, minivans, and tour buses carry 20th-century visitors to Bonaventure. Tiny traffic jams are not uncommon on the weekends. People from around the world, on vacation in Savannah, come to explore this famous cemetery. (Photo taken April 1998.)

These serene images are from stereographs. The beauty and peacefulness has inspired many sightseers over the years to wax poetic. Numerous poems have found their way into newspapers, magazines, and various pamphlets.

Tree-lined vistas such as this are part of Bonaventure's fascination. These avenues almost ask to be explored. Unfortunately, Bonaventure's peaceful reverie has been disrupted in recent years. In 1989 and 1990 a rash of vandalism struck many local cemeteries, including Bonaventure and Greenwich. Gravestones were toppled, new graves and floral arrangements were disturbed, and the Mongin vault (page 71) had bones stolen. As a result, "No trespassing after dark" signs were posted, and night security patrols at Greenwich were increased. Additionally, a new gate, that is locked at five o'clock every night, was installed at the entrance.

Originally built as the caretaker's house, this brick building is now home to the Visitor's Center and the cemetery office. The Bonaventure Historical Society, which runs the Visitor's Center, was founded in 1994 under the leadership of Terry Shaw and Margaret DeBolt, current chairman and vice chairperson respectfully. Originally known as the Friends of Bonaventure, the society is "dedicated to the evolution and preservation of Bonaventure as a historical, educational site." They publish an informational map for visitors, research the history of people who are buried there, maintain plots, and conduct tours. Recently, the Bonaventure Historical Society has received city approval to name the streets in the cemetery. The illustration (below) was designed by George Tassey Jr. and is the logo that appears on the society's newsletter (used by permission).

Terry Shaw
Editor & Author

George Tassey, Jr.
Graphics & Layout

Bonaventure 1846

Bonaventure Historical Society
Volume 4, No. 4, January 1998

One of the difficulties facing the cemetery and the Bonaventure Historical Society is striking a balance between maintaining the integrity of the cemetery and the volumes of people who want to visit this historic site. To help accomplish this, the Bonaventure Historical Society has developed educational programs. Through their efforts, perhaps visitors will realize the historical significance of the area and act accordingly. Although the local tour companies' buses (seen above and below) may seem incongruous with the peacefulness of the cemetery, for every one bus, approximately five cars are eliminated from the traffic flow, thus lessening the amount of congestion. (Photos taken April 1998.)

Sandwiched between Bonaventure and Greenwich is the Forest Lawn Memory Gardens. Organized in 1955, Forest Lawn is in sharp contrast to the trees and monuments of the two older cemeteries. Designed for ease of maintenance, no tombstones are permitted, only ground level bronze name plates. Although maintenance may be easier, uniformity is stressed. Gone is the individuality that is expressed through monuments and memorials, the tender touches of bittersweet epitaphs or carefully planted shrubbery. (Photos taken April 1998.)

Tradition lives on in Bonaventure. Besides the Greenwich addition, Bonaventure has new sections that accommodate more recent burials. Although these sections look more contemporary and burials must follow modern regulations, their monuments and gravestones continue the eclectic feel of the historic sections. (Photos taken April 1998.)

125

The white marble monument at the Baldwin grave (Section H, lot 39) speaks to the hearts of visitors—"Verily I say unto you whosoever shall not receive the Kingdom of God as a little child he shall not enter therein," (Mark's Gospel, chapter 10, verse 15). The Baldwin monument is one of many marble reminders of the earthly lives of those who slumber beneath the branches of Bonaventure. The silent beauty of this cemetery is not soon forgotten.

INDEX